I Called Her Nan is beautiful. Really. I'm not sure anyone has explored the mother in-law relationship in such a positive way aside from Ruth and Naomi! What a wonderful gift this would make for every bride!

Amy Lyle, Author

This is a fresh topic that so many women struggle with. The author, Cathy Lopes, shares her challenges from her first encounter with her mother-in-law to today with her own daughters-in-law. She is candid, honest, and vulnerable. This book is thought provoking and is sure to make you stop and reflect on your own relationships, whether they are good or bad.

Kim Kirkby, Chesapeake, VA.

A mother-in-law is a special person. Whether easy to get along with or more difficult, whether totally accepting or not as accepting, whether called by a pet name or by Mrs. her last name, she is special because she is the mother of the one you love and married. Each reader who has a mother-in-law will connect with various aspects of this book, just as I did. Reading *I Called Her Nan* brought back a flood of memories of my mother-in law. As I read, I often thought I was reading our story, as many parts resonated deeply with me. You will be touched in so many ways as you read this wonderful memoir.

Linda Warren, Retired English teacher,
Great Bridge High School, Chesapeake VA

I am the mom of 8 daughters and 2 sons. I homeschool 7 of them and 3 are grown with their own families. I didn't get along enough with my mother-in-law but I can tell you one thing—I loved and respected her because of my relationship with my husband. I loved him by loving her. It is my message to my married daughters today. If you are in any doubt of how important this is, you have found the book for you. Cathy shares so many personal stories and how they can help anyone walking this journey do so with grace, understanding, and care. I know it will change your life for the better. It did for me!

Sharon, Hartwell, Ga

Having known Cathy and her family for many years, some of *I Called Her Nan* was familiar, but I still learned a lot as I read and pictured the stories being told. I could hear Cathy's voice as she spoke her words of wisdom earned throughout the years. I connected with a lot of what she shared, as I have a strong desire to have a close knit family and find having family spread out among several states a challenge. While most of this book is dedicated to the relationships between mothers and daughters-in-law, the insights I have gained will most definitely be a benefit to me as a mother-in-law to my daughter's new husband and will guide me to help my daughter as she develops a healthy relationship with her husband's mother.

Debbie, Hershey, PA

I Called Her
Nan

The Journey from
Daughter-in-law to Mother-in-law

Cathy Randolph Lopes

Self-Published in Atlanta, Georgia

ISBN: 978-0-578-68364-5

Printed in the United States of America

Library of Congress Cataloguing-in-Publication Data

This book is dedicated to my
mother-in-law,
Marion "Babe" Lopes

Contents

In Memory Of Marion "Babe" Lopes

To write this poem, I needed a place to start,
    So, I closed my eyes and felt the words just flow from my heart.
To some she was known as Marion. To others, Babe was her name.
    The grandchildren called her Nanny. Will you play a game?
Her nickname was given to her many years ago,
    By her Daddy who loved her so.
Mama she was called by her three sons,
    For they were her life. They were her precious ones.
Her husband called her Darlin for 45 years.
    They had a wonderful life and their share of tears.
Her door was always open when you came her way,
    and the sheets would be pulled back if you needed to stay.
She chose a career of physical therapy to lend a hand,
    touching people and helping them until they could stand.
She volunteered her time in so many ways,
    like bringing others food and brightening up their days.
The library was her favorite place to go,
    she loved to read, as we all know.
Now we dedicate this bench to you,
    Marion "Babe" Lopes.
So, others can rest, laugh, talk,
    and share their hopes.
This bench is a reminder of who you are,
    a daughter, wife, mother, nanny, and friend.
Our memories and love for you will never end.
To my mother-in-law whom I called Nan-
    until we meet again, on the other side.

April 2000

Introduction

As women, we are all someone's daughter. We fall in love, get married, then become a daughter-in-law. We have children, they fall in love and get married, then... we become a mother-in-law. It's a role that doesn't usually hold a high priority and at times can be a sensitive subject for various reasons. Throughout history and in many homes, it isn't thought of as a significant relationship except during times of indifference and miscommunication. Nothing brought these two women together in most cases, except for the son. The common string that ties them together is the love of one person.

I am not a writer but I do know our Father who is the author of life. He is my mentor and has placed on my heart to put into words how much He values mothers-in- law and daughters-in-law relationships.

An example of this relationship in the Bible can be found in the book of Ruth. This story comes with many heartaches, trials, determination, and sacrifices for both Ruth and Naomi. Their different cultures set them apart, but the son/husband brought them together. Over time, their unexplainable devotion created blessings that came pouring into their lives, which resonated for generations to come. Here you will find the lineage of Christ.

I am writing this book with the understanding of a daughter-in-law and the heart of a mother-in-law. Its intention is not to point out faults or pity but to establish new eyes for future relationships. It's to encourage you to take the time and sit with each other early on to create your opinion of who this woman is that fell in love with your son and who the woman is that raised your future husband. I have prayed over this subject for many years, even before I had a daughter-in-law of my own. My mother-in-law once told me, "I picked you." I didn't give it much thought back then but found her words sweet and complimenting. I see differently now, for his mom was sharing a piece of her heart with me.

My mother-in-law had three sons. I married the youngest. I also have three sons who have given me three daughters-in-law, whom I've grown to adore.

My husband Jeff and I have raised three boys, Oryan, Morgan, and Jordan. They were always flexible in the many moves we made over the years in hopes of providing them with opportunities for a prosperous future.

We are proud of the choices they made in reference to their teenage years, educational decisions, and especially, when they chose their wives. The anticipation of growing our family was exciting for all of us! My first thought was: Yay! I am going to have a daughter(s)! She is going to love me like I loved my mother-in-law!

Little did I know, that slipping into Nan's shoes was putting me on a path of seasons with hills and valleys. I didn't know that her shoes got wet by her tears from the silent storms she weathered only to be dried by the rays of sun that peeked through on any given day. My journey was about to begin...

After Nan's death, I started journaling every once in a while. Once we moved to Georgia from Virginia, it turned into writing a little more every day. They were simple entries about our daily activities and Bible verses that stood out to me. It helped me with the transition of moving away from my close friends and a job that I enjoyed. My morning quiet time strengthened me for each new day.

Over the past few years, I began looking back over my journals and noticed how my writing had changed over time. While reading the old entries, I often caught myself saying, "I wish I'd figured that out sooner." I realized that if I had known then what I know now, it would have made a difference in how I responded to people or saw others, especially my three daughters-in-law.

I'll share this interaction as an example of when I started to learn the importance of communicating more effectively with these young women.

We were in the den of my home when I started picking up my granddaughter Adelaide's toys. Danielle, Oryan's wife, was sitting on the couch and said, "I'll get those."

I told her, "It's no problem. I'm right here. I'll pick them up."

She said, "I said I'll get them."

I stopped, sat back on the floor, and thought to myself, "Why does she find fault in everything I say or do?"

I replayed it to myself to hear how I said it. Then it dawned on me that maybe she heard what I said in a different way. After a moment of gathering my thoughts, I gave Danielle this example: "We agreed ahead of time that I would come by your house to drop off dinner, because you were getting home late from work. While I was there, I folded the clothes lying on the couch and I ran the vacuum that was sitting out. How would that make you feel?"

She responded by saying, "I would have felt like you thought my house was dirty!"

There was an aha moment! I explained to her that when Nan did those things for me on occasions, I loved it since I worked outside of the home full time and the boys had evening activities. I enjoyed coming home to the little things being done. It was so helpful, just as if my own mom had done it for me. It was at that moment that we realized where most of our miscommunication came from. We both did not hear or see the same way on certain subjects due to our different lifestyles. We really did not know how each other's thought processes worked. Our stage of lives, backgrounds, and generational gap had caused friction between us over five years, which led us to feel hurt or frustrated with each other over simple things. Never mind the tension Oryan must have felt with his wife and mother not being able to get along.

Danielle and I talked for a good while that afternoon. I pointed out that as a parent and investing so much time into our children and their accomplishments over the years, I would not intentionally cause discord between them and the women they have chosen to create their own home and family. Especially when I see my children so happy.

Since then, we have tried to communicate better. We realize that it is ok to ask instead of assuming that we understand the intent of something that was said or the way something was done.

It was this disconnect between my intention and her reaction that led me to write this book in an effort to help other mothers-in-law and daughters-in-law think about how the other perceives their interactions.

1

Meeting His Mom

My story begins at fifteen years old in the small town of Great Bridge, in Virginia. I was a sophomore when I met Jeff, my future husband, in our high school library during the winter of 1981. He would come to the library during his study hall and sit at a table where he could see me when he looked up. I had long blonde hair and was very shy. I worked behind the counter and helped students check out books. Finally, one day his friend who sat with him came up to me and said, "That guy over there likes you." After the bell rang, Jeff stopped on his way out while I was filing books away. He introduced himself and handed me a red lollipop with a white cupid and heart on it and said, "I got this for you." He smiled and headed out the door to his next class.

Later that spring, we started going out. Jeff took me to his home in the country where they had horses and chickens along with a goat named Sweet Pea. The house was an old white concrete ranch with red shutters. There was a white barn out back with red doors. The horses were roaming in the pasture, and an above ground pool under a big shade tree looked inviting. In between the clothesline near the chain-linked fence and the shade tree sat an old burn barrel with smoke billowing out. I noticed that his country home was different than mine in the suburbs.

When we pulled into the gravel driveway, the garage door was open, and a truck was parked with the hood up. A stocky man peered around from under the hood and said, "Hello, Darlin," in his northern accent. Then he went back to work. That was my first encounter with Art, Jeff's dad. He was different than my dad.

As we went to the backyard, the metal gate no sooner clinked shut than I looked up and saw a woman hanging out clothes. It was his mom. She was in her late forties, tall, wearing shorts, a white tank top, and boots that stopped at her calf. Her hair was short, and her skin showed that she enjoyed the sun. A warm smile lit up her face when she saw us as she shouted, "Hi they-a!" in her northern accent. She dropped the clothing into the basket on the ground and walked over to greet us. I didn't know that just seeing her son brought her joy. She was different from my mom.

Mentioning that his home and parents were different than mine is not to imply that they were better or worse, for I love my parents. But it is to point out that everyone's parents, homes, and lifestyles are different. It's a chance for you to relate to the subjects that will be touched upon throughout these pages. If you are reading this book, you'll see that your story has actually begun. It will unfold in the years to come.

His mom offered us cheese and crackers with sweet tea on the back porch that was painted red like the shutters and the barn doors. I didn't know that she loved to serve. But I did notice that her tea tasted a bit strange and the crackers were on the stale side. I didn't know that they had well water, which gave the tea a unique taste. I also didn't know that she bought items in bulk since she lived so far from a store, which resulted in stale cookies and crackers at times. I really didn't give it much thought at all, I just wanted to hang out with Jeff. So, I ate the cheese and crackers and drank the sweet tea. We swam and floated in the pool that afternoon. When it was time to leave, I said "Goodbye, Mrs. Lopes!" Her nickname was Babe— I didn't know.

I bring up "I didn't know" moments because I was a young girl and of course, my eyes were set on the boy. Later, I would learn through life experiences where else to set my eyes, yet at the time, I just didn't know. My hope is that you'll soon see it with your heart.

Be patient in understanding the woman who raised the man you love. Be likewise to the young woman who loves your boy.

Jeff and I hung out a lot that summer, investing time into each other's lives and learning things that were important to each other. We listened to REO Speed Wagon music on our long rides to the country. Although the ride was only twenty-five minutes, it felt longer as we drove through cornfields and curvy roads. Sometimes we rode in his dad's Ford truck. It was baby blue with a thick white stripe down the side. I would sit in the middle of the bench seat, holding Jeff's hand. It was the best of times!

Over the next few months, I was in the country more often. I found myself floating in the pool with his mom who smoked cigarettes and drank beer with tomato juice! She had a raspy, New England voice and a hearty laugh. She would talk about skinny dipping at night with Jeff's dad! No details, but the mental vision was enough. Unknown to me at the time was how much she enjoyed reading all kinds of books! She went to the library often and even volunteered there for many years. Outside the Pungo library in Virginia Beach, there sits a beautiful teak bench in honor of her service. The poem at the beginning of this book was read during the dedication of that bench on a warm spring day.

I could have easily thought of our conversations as strange since they were unlike any topics I had discussed before, most likely stemming from all the books she read. But I chose, without even realizing it, to see her as unique, funny, and interesting. In a way, she was simple. It would be years later that I would learn that simple is good. It was peaceful.

His mom was a physical therapist. Once in a while, I went with her to the hospital where she worked on a Saturday morning once a month. She knew I wanted to be a nurse, so she offered me this opportunity to be inside a hospital. It was also a chance to stay the night at her house since we had to get up so early and drive forty-five minutes to the hospital. After eating breakfast in the cafeteria, we would get a wheelchair to pick up her first patient.

I remember how the patients loved to see her and smiled when she walked into their rooms. She called them by name, and they called her, Marion. I watched her bathe their wounds and laugh at their jokes. I noticed how she charted her notes carefully for each patient. That image stayed with me once I became a nurse.

I thought those Saturdays with her were about me. But once I grew to see differently, I realized it was a blessing for me to be able to see her outside of being a mom and her country life. I got a glimpse of a professional woman. It also gave me a chance to see where Jeff got his gentle spirit and kindness for others.

2

Time Apart

Well, Jeff and I broke up at Christmas time that year. I think I was too much of a proper city girl for him at the time— which is another whole story! A good example of God's timing, not ours. Looking back, I'm grateful for that time apart.

One summer day while we were broken up, I found myself missing Jeff, so I took a drive through the country. I passed his house, hoping he wouldn't see my car go by. I joyfully noticed that his car wasn't there. In a split second, I decided to see if his mom was home to say hi. So, I turned around in the driveway and pulled up on the opposite side of the house so that if Jeff came home, he wouldn't see that I was visiting his mom. That would have been totally awkward! I was driving a blue Gremlin back then, and you couldn't miss that, so I couldn't stay long.

His mom greeted me at the door with a hug. It was her afternoon reading and nap time, so we laid on her sloshy waterbed where she enjoyed reading. She reached over her head and pulled out a stash of dark chocolate from the wooden headboard shelf. She handed me a piece and said, "This will make you feel better." I think she could tell I had been crying over her boy. His mom offered me advice. "If you love someone, set them free, and they'll come back if it's meant to be." For some reason, that made me feel hopeful at the time. But I now know to say, "If it's God's will." To this day, I still enjoy this memory, along with a piece of dark chocolate.

It was one of many simple moments with his mom. It's a clear example that once we start to see and listen differently, little things do matter. Time spent with someone is never wasted. God will use it according to His will and in His time. Even a simple word of encouragement to give hope and a piece of dark chocolate doesn't go to waste!

By now you are likely able to plug in your own story of when you first met his mom. The first encounter is usually a casual meeting when you are dating. You may have met at a restaurant or at an event. In some cases, you met at her home. Yet some of you may have known his family for years and cannot recall that exact moment you met his mother. But once you start to love the boy, that is the beginning of a new relationship. The love of the boy is your "Hello." As simple as it may sound, you just met the woman who raised the man you love. Without realizing it, his mom slips back and waits, all the while enjoying watching her son be happy with his new love, understanding that his heart could get broken yet also knowing that this girl could be the one to bring him joy. The one to share his life.

A mother raises her son to leave. As a young woman, I didn't consider his mother's heart or her position of raising and letting go of a child. It wasn't my season in life to fully understand. But through time, I have learned the process of letting go. It begins when they are young. Little by little, they leave us by becoming more independent and making decisions on their own. That is a good thing.

If he's in an unhealthy relationship, you pray that your child seeks your opinion or uses the judgment of his own heart and upbringing in knowing right from wrong. Ultimately, he is the one to make decisions for himself once he is an adult. Only he knows the depth of his love for this other person. It's not about you any longer. Just like it wasn't about me as I let each of my own boys go. It's about encouraging your son to make his own good decisions.

As parents, we need to trust that we did the best that we could. Surely there are times that we wished we did or said some things differently. Perhaps we will never know how God used even those moments to shape our children.

3

Wedding Bells

Jeff and I eventually got back together after he graduated from High School, and we dated through my Senior year. He proposed the night I graduated from High School on a dirt path called Back Road in our town. I was seventeen years old. Even though I was caught off guard and quite surprised, I said yes!

I was nineteen years old when I planned my wedding. Clueless is the word that comes to mind. I wasn't familiar with a lot of styles or traditions of a wedding. I remember feeling irritable at times with so much to do and the cost. Yet it all worked out in the end. Looking back, I see there were opportunities to have extra helping hands along the way. Although my mom helped the best she could, I also remember hearing my future mother-in-law asking if she could help. I didn't consider that she was an only child or her own mother had already passed away. She just raised three boys, and although two of them were already married, I didn't wonder if she had experienced taking part in any special wedding moments. I didn't accept her help. Nor did I ask for it. I don't even recall sharing the details of the wedding with her, which could have been as simple as a lunch date. To have given one hour of my time with the woman that gave me the man I would love for years to come, it would have made her feel special and included. However, I do recall her showing up to my shower and bringing practical gifts that were needed to start a home. Some of those items I still use today.

A realization: In most cases, the future daughter-in-law does not need another mother. The bride is ready to create her own home and traditions. They seek their own mothers and girlfriends to share in the excitement, opinions, and planning of the big day.

Another realization: Some girls do not have their mother close by or may have a strained relationship due to a broken home. She may be a foster child without any family roots. Some brides no longer have their mothers living or involved in their lives. These are facts that deserve mentioning because everyone's situation varies. Planning a wedding is such a busy time, so much to do, and yet so much to learn along the way for both women.

Once Jeff and I were married, I had a personal dilemma, sort of awkward actually. I didn't know what to call my mother-in-law. Looking back, this would have been a fun subject to discuss and figure out ahead of time— maybe over that lunch, I spoke about earlier. The name Mrs. Lopes seemed too formal. Babe was too casual. Marion didn't seem to fit. So, I chose not to call her by any name at all! I wonder if she even noticed.

For me, I enjoy hearing my daughters-in-law call me by my name or the nickname they found for me, Bebop. It is their way of saying, "This woman never stops, or this woman hops from one thing to another." Of course, they could have been thinking, "This woman is crazy!" But if that's how they see me at times, so be it.

4

Boy Oh Boy Oh Boy

Jeff and I consider ourselves good people. We try to treat others with respect and do the right things in life. I grew up Catholic, and Jeff occasionally attended a Baptist church. Neither one of us grew up reading the Bible, yet we knew of a few stories and believed in God. We knew there were different religions but did not invest too much time into our actual faith. It wouldn't be until much later that we learned about having a relationship with Christ and how different it was than a religion. Over the years, that relationship would direct our steps.

Expecting our first baby was so exciting! Oh yes, another clueless time for us, or at least for me. There were not many baby books out in the eighties. Even though there were a few, we did not read any of them. There was no internet access to pull up for quick questions or baby ideas. Yet like before, love was the common bond that Jeff and I had for our new little person. We didn't think about praying over this new life, although we were grateful for a healthy child.

A realization: we would later learn that God had a plan for each of us. It's usually not what you would expect.

Throughout the coming years, He would redirect our eyes toward Him and show us more than just a good life. He would show us an abundant life. This took longer than an overnight adventure. It's a growing process, and we were getting ready to have growing pains and joys.

In my early twenties, our first son, Oryan, was born. Fifteen short months later, our second son, Morgan, came along. When he was eight weeks old, we moved away from friends and family for a job opportunity in North Carolina for Jeff. Shortly after moving, we realized the job wasn't a fit and his true desire was to teach. So, eighteen months later, we returned to our hometown, for Jeff to go back to school for an education degree. Then during the busiest time in our lives, while Jeff was a Senior in college, waiting tables at a hotel restaurant and I was working full time, our third son, Jordan, was born. The boys are known to this day as O, Mo, and Jo. Jeff and I can truly say that they have been the greatest joys in our lives and our proudest accomplishments together.

Once we had a child, my dilemma on what to call my mother-in-law was resolved! She was already being called Nanny by the older grandchildren, so we followed that lead. Our boys went along and called her Nanny. It was also close to the name Nana, which Jeff called his maternal grandmother whom he had fond memories of visiting.

It didn't take long until I found myself shortening Nanny down to Nan when I spoke to her. It was wonderful calling her by a name that seemed to fit, and from then on, I called her Nan.

5

Stay a Little Longer

Most of my conversations about life and death with Nan involved her vision of reincarnation. Yet she believed in God. Although our beliefs were different, I never actually thought of dying and eternity personally. I just knew that I believed in God and heaven's existence.

Things suddenly changed on October 31, 1999. It was a Sunday morning. My father-in-law called me and said, "Babe is sick and acting strange."

I got to their home close to lunchtime and found her on the bed flipping through the yellow pages. I asked, "Nan, what are you doing? What's wrong?"

She looked up at me and said that she was looking for a doctor to see the next day. When she tried to get up, I noticed that she was unsteady, clammy, and pale. Art said that she has been thirsty and drinking a lot. I thought that she may be diabetic and told her that she needed to go to the ER. She refused as hard as I persisted. I finally said, "Look, it's Halloween, and I need to get home and help Jeff with the boys. Plus, Art is worried, and you don't feel well."

I didn't mention it before, but Nan was a strong-willed woman. To use the expression "she was boss" would be accurate. She did not go to the doctor unless she was really sick. I seldom heard her complain, so the thought of her developing diabetes would not have surprised me. She also coughed for as long as I'd known her, but since she enjoyed her cigarettes, we left that subject alone. Finally, she agreed to go to the hospital with Art that afternoon. I went home to trick or treat with the boys, all while having an unsettled feeling in the pit of my stomach.

As life often does, it catches us off guard at times. She was admitted for testing. During her hospital stay that week, one of the x-rays revealed a mass in her chest. It was Friday, November 5th when she had a procedure that revealed stage IV lung cancer. It had already spread to her major organs. I was there listening to the doctor explain this type of cancer to Jeff's dad. We were both waiting for her to come out of recovery. I remember the sensation in my ears of the muffled sound of my father-in-law crying above the doctor's words. All along, my mind was whirling with questions. As a nurse, her symptoms over the past few months came rushing into my mind. How did I not see this coming? If she were my own mother, would I have noticed her symptoms or asked more questions? Would I have encouraged her to see a doctor sooner? Or in the long run, would it have changed the outcome?

Cancer—I had to tell Jeff his mom had inoperable lung cancer. There were no cell phones at this time, so he had to wait until I could get to him to let him know the results of her test. I drove to the school where he taught and waited in the lobby on a cold metal bench until it was lunchtime for his class. While sitting there, I realized that I never had someone this close to me so sick. What would it be like caring for her? For it was never a question in my mind whether or not I would be there for her since she did not have a daughter of her own. I found myself wondering what life would be like without this woman.

I wish I could say that my faith allowed me to be still and pray for my husband, but instead, my thoughts were all over the place. Soon, the bell rang for the kids to go to lunch. I got up and slowly walked to Jeff's class. As I walked into his classroom, he sat on the corner of his desk as if to prepare himself for what I had to say. I remember telling him it wasn't good news and explained the diagnosis the best I could. He hung his head and cried. Leaving him alone afterward was one of the hardest things I have ever done. He finished the school day, and honestly, I cannot recall the rest of that afternoon.

A few days later, Nan was discharged from the hospital and wanted to go home to the country. She thanked the doctor for his care and said that she would not be back. When I tried to persuade her to try chemotherapy, she said, "Get her out of here." I knew then that her mind was made up not to have treatment. Although I wanted her to stay with us a little longer, I knew we had to honor her wishes. Therefore, I helped her pack up to leave.

While I pushed her wheelchair down the hospital hallway, it was clear that our lives were about to change. Once outside, Jeff and I helped her into the car without saying another word since it was my desire to be with her until the end. As the car door started to shut, I heard Art clear his throat as he said, "Come on, Darlin." I stood there as they drove away. He was taking Babe home.

We chose not to tell the boys about Nanny's illness until her health started fading quickly. Looking back, I'm not sure that was the best decision, but at the time, that's what we decided. During the whole month of November, the days were spent juggling our family, working life, and caring for Nan's needs along with preparing Jeff's dad for the changes to come.

At the time, I had two days off a week. On those days, I would get the boys off to school and drive straight to the country. I spent most of those days with her just lying on the bed. I started thinking about her feelings. How would I feel if it was me with cancer? I knew that I would be afraid, not wanting to be alone. So, in the quiet room, I would help her drink iced coffee, which is all she wanted. I would clip her nails and rub her arms and legs. Warm towels on her body helped with the itching that the cancer was causing. There were times when I felt like I needed to speak with her about heaven, but I didn't have the words to share. What faith or hope did I have that could bring her comfort?

One day in the stillness, while I was lying next to her on the little double bed in the yellow-painted guest room, warm tears were rolling down my cheeks as I listened to her ragged breathing. I didn't want her to hear me cry, yet there was a pressure I felt inside of me, knowing there was more I wanted to tell her! As if she knew what I could not say, I felt her cool hand reach over and rest upon mine. Ever so gently, she patted my hand to bring *me* comfort with just her touch.

6

Can You Hear Me?

I remember thinking that this woman who cares for people and animals cannot just leave. The impact she made on those around her could not go to waste. The uncertainty of what to say during my time with her sparked an interest to learn more about God and heaven. It started with general conversations with God. I guess you could say, I started praying. It became different than just reciting words. Soon, a desire to read the Bible crept into my heart. Looking back, I see how each step was created for me to learn through Nan's illness. There are many moments in all of our lives where we are given opportunities to seek His kingdom, our eternal home. It's our own choice to draw closer to Him during these times. Through the gift of free will, we are able to choose the path for our own lives and eternity.

It was the Sunday evening after Thanksgiving, my mom came to our house to watch the boys while Jeff and I went to his parents' house. On the ride to the country, I felt a tug in my heart. It actually felt like a sadness where, once again, tears fell without crying. When we arrived at the little country house, I walked straight to her room while Jeff talked to his brother and father in the den. I knelt down next to her bed and saw that her breathing was irregular like she was puffing out the air between inhaling. I heard the water running in the bathroom and knew Art was starting to take his evening shower. As I took Nan's hand in mine, I started to pray the only prayer I could think of which was the Hail Mary. Afterward, I found myself whispering, "Nan, can you hear me? I love you." Words that could have been spoken throughout the years, were now the last words for her to hear from me. As her eyes clicked open, and her last breath made a long fading sound, all I could say was, "Nan, can you hear me? I love you."

On this side of eternity, that was the last time I called her Nan.

7

On the Move

Less than two years after Nan died as our oldest child was starting high school, we decided to move to Georgia. Jeff and the boys were ready for a change, and this was the best time to go for it! Thus, we sold our home, packed up our belongings into two moving trucks, and loaded down my van. It was a weird feeling seeing my stuff going down I- 85 south with a child in each vehicle. Morgan drove with Art in the small truck while Oryan drove in the big truck with Jeff. Jordan and our dog Rascal drove with me. I was grateful that he was so young and played in the back seat. I didn't want him to see me crying as we drove away or hear the sniffles that lasted most of the nine-hour road trip. But something was telling me that this was the right decision, so I went along with my gut feeling and left everything familiar behind in Virginia.

My brother Randy was already living in Georgia, which made the move a bit easier. Jeff found a teaching job fairly easily, yet I struggled to find a fit in my nursing career. I loved my job in Virginia and was homesick for my girlfriends. I definitely missed the day to day girl interactions, which included lots of laughing over silly things! I was lonely, and I would have loved to pick up the phone to chat with Nan. I think she would have understood how I felt.

From the moment we arrived in Georgia, we hit the ground running with baseball and school. Some of you may be able to relate to how busy life can be with children in extracurricular activities. It was actually fun, and we all were eventually thriving in our new town of Suwanee, even me! We found a great church home, which provided the boys a chance to do various mission projects in other states, which Jeff and I participated in whenever we could. We all grew in our faith during those years. I started to find some women who I could relate to and enjoyed going to women's Bible studies, something I had never done before. It kept me craving to learn more about the stories in the Bible.

Over the years, chaperoning youth trips was actually one of my favorite things to do. I found the energy from the sixty-plus kids invigorating as we traveled on a charter bus, and the people we met in other states were inspiring. In the poorest areas, there was something new to hear and see outside of my own world. Something new to learn each day. Waking up in different states was exciting— from a college dorm in Chicago to an old hotel in Queens, New York. I would rise before the kids to walk the streets in the early morning hours for coffee, bagels, or doughnuts. Even feeling the mist from Niagara Falls sparked a sense of awe. It dawned on me: Would this life and time with our boys have been possible if we had never taken the chance and moved? I wondered if this was part of that gut feeling I had all along.

The boys developed close friendships within the church youth group. Most of these relationships have continued throughout the years, even into their adult lives. The teenage girls who came into my life allowed me to see what having a daughter would have been like. They laughed with me, cried over boys at times, yet most of the guys were like brothers to them. They would sit with me on the bus and flop on my bed during youth trips. I also found that most teenage girls (like the boys) do not keep a tidy bath-room—just saying. On occasions, they stayed in the guest room of our home and showered me with hugs too numerous to count. To say I love these girls is an understatement! Even at their young age, they made an impression on me.

8

In Nan's Shoes—My Journey Begins

Being the mother of three boys, the thought of having a daughter-in-law brought much excitement and anticipation. As I mentioned before, since I was active in the youth group, my experiences with the girls was one of hugs, carefree chatting, and being included in activities. There was a sit on the bed conversation with a special young lady that I still hold dear to this day. At that moment, there was a flashback from over many years ago. Except for this time, it was me on the other side. I didn't just remember the words on the sloshy water bed with Nan but I felt them. I actually felt my mother-in-law's heart during my conversation with this young lady. It was a new feeling. I guess you could call it the first aha moment. There was a swell of emotions inside of me as to what else I did not see in her. What else did she feel? I let those questions get tucked away in my mind due to a lack of understanding. In the years to come, I would soon see and feel more clearly what it means to walk in someone else's shoes. But even at forty, I didn't know…yet.

A few years later, in what seemed like the blink of an eye, I took the first steps on the path of becoming a mother-in-law.

Danielle

I met Danielle at Homecoming and the Ring Ceremony during Oryan's senior year in college at The Citadel in South Carolina. At the time, she had short curly hair and looked cute as a little girl yet at the same time beautiful like a young woman in a formal dress. Her smile gave me a warm feeling and a sense of uncertainty as she introduced her parents Ralph and Kathy to me and Jeff, for we were used to knowing most of the boys' friends and parents. Yet here we were meeting an Italian family from New Jersey whom we knew nothing about except that they lived many miles away from our Georgia home and their daughter liked our son.

After the Ring Ceremony and a little dancing at the school, we all headed to dinner at a local Charleston restaurant. It was there that I noticed some differences in our families, although I didn't give it much attention. I learned quickly that mealtime can be a festive event for Italians! That evening, I enjoyed listening about a variety of wines and food dishes and how they are prepared and presented their meals.

It wasn't long before Oryan brought Danielle home to meet everyone else in our family and spend a weekend away from school. We were having spaghetti night, the perfect Italian dish! Or so I thought. I was unaware that her parents made their own spaghetti sauce from fresh tomatoes and their own sausage links from scratch. Of course, had I known, I would have chosen a different menu, maybe something more southern! But she was gracious and ate the jarred spaghetti sauce, which I doctored up, along with the store-bought garlic bread.

As we sat around and chatted, I couldn't help but notice how Oryan was beaming throughout the evening. I could tell that he was proud of Danielle and was glad he brought her home. I knew my boy had fallen in love. It was a sweet weekend.

After dating the following year, they got engaged after graduation. Due to my son's military schedule, the wedding was planned for four months later in New Jersey! I started wondering who would be able to drive so far to attend? Our family was in Virginia and our church friends were in Georgia. We had also hoped that the boys' youth Pastor Brian could marry them.

The next few months we were busy preparing and making arrangements to travel for the wedding. Once there, I was so happy to be included in helping to set up for the reception and being part of getting ready for the wedding with the bridal party. It felt so nice to have one of her friends offer to fix my hair and touch up my makeup. It may sound like a simple thing, but to a mother of all boys, it was a treat I'll always remember.

We managed to work it out so Brian could fly to New Jersey to perform the wedding ceremony. He shared a room with Art. Brian has his own story to tell about that adventure, but in the end, they both became friends. The ceremony was one to be remembered. Danielle and Oryan looked so happy. Some of our dearest friends drove from Virginia and Georgia for the wedding, which meant so much to us. I don't think there was a dry eye in the room during the whole ceremony. It was a beautiful wedding, and the reception was a true Italian event, which we all enjoyed as we ate and danced the night away!

It wasn't long before Danielle and I started feeling a tension between us. It mostly started during Oryan's first deployment to Afghanistan. Although we lived in different states, we managed to disagree about certain things when it came to Oryan. You see, I never knew the anxiety that went along with having a child deployed during wartime. My heart hurt so bad at times I could not breathe from worrying. While all along Danielle was newly married, and her husband had left for seven months. When most newlyweds are together, setting up house, Danielle found herself married and living in a strange town alone. Our lack of understanding and not really knowing each other caused poor communication at times and hurt feelings. I wish I could say that we figured it out quickly, but we did not. The tension was uncomfortable for years to come.

When my first grandchild Adelaide was born, Oryan was on his second deployment. It was important for Jeff and me to be there when she arrived, hoping this brought Oryan some peace that his wife had extra support. Plus, it was our first grandchild, and we didn't want to miss seeing her arrival into the world! After packing up quickly, we drove seven hours to the North Carolina hospital. We were so excited! It worked out that our other boys Jordan and Morgan along with his wife Megan were able to come the following day. Looking back, here is where we could see God's hand clearly at work showing us the importance of families coming together to share in joyous occasions! But that joy for us all was short-lived. Danielle had major complications after the delivery and had to be airlifted to another hospital an hour and a half away. The Red Cross had called Oryan home, but it would take him days to arrive. Danielle being transported to another hospital left me with this new child who had yet to be held by her own mother. In my heart, I titled this time "Loving Adie." Over that weekend, both sets of new grandparents, along with Mo, Meg, Jo, and Dom (Danielle's sister) rocked, fed, and loved Adie through our touch and soft kisses. Within a few days, Danielle miraculously started recovering, and Adelaide was finally placed in her mother's arms where she belonged. Kathy and I stood silently and watched while Danielle unwrapped her baby, inspecting her fingers and toes then gently laid Adelaide on her chest, kissed her cheek, and closed her eyes.

Oryan arrived home four days later to his baby girl and wife. As grandparents, Ralph, Kathy, Jeff, and I knew the memory of this time together would never be forgotten.

It still took Danielle and me a few years to figure out how to communicate better. Each visit, we talked more and more as she became at ease with a house full of boys, and I learned to be at ease with her. She has learned to hide her food at our house if she's planning on preparing it for a meal along with getting herself a serving of something before it's gone! This is an example of an area of frustration that has now been replaced with laughter. Now, we both hide the food or the treats we want for ourselves! Every once in a while, we'll hear, "Ya'll think you're smart, don't you?" Yep, the guys would find our stash!

Danielle and I have learned a lot about each other over the years. We actually took a cross-country road trip together a few years ago when she was headed back to California before Oryan came home from his third deployment. She had split her time between both parents while he was away that summer. Those days on the road with her and Adie were priceless. Nothing like driving hundreds of miles and stopping at every rest area to pee in the southwestern desert to spark unique conversations! Danielle is an example of endurance and sacrifice. She is a military wife. I was proud to drive the dry desert road back with her that summer as we headed to another temporary town and house that she made into their home.

Megan

Two short years later, Megan came into our lives. I laid eyes on her for the first time on a Sunday morning in church. Jeff and I drove to Atlanta to meet Morgan and some of his friends. While hugging my boy, I noticed a young woman with the most beautiful red hair I've ever seen watching us. Her smile was warm and her green eyes were friendly. We all enjoyed the service and agreed to meet for lunch afterward. As Jeff and I were walking into the restaurant, he said, "Don't say a word." We both laughed, knowing the feeling we got from Meg was mutual. We could tell she was a strong woman by the way she carried herself and spoke. She seemed like someone who would complement Mo's personality yet keep things straight. And, she liked his long hair! We ate our lunch outside on the patio and enjoyed each other's company. Mo had another friend join us. We could tell he liked Megan too! Oh, but who would eventually win her affection? Mo did, and Jeff and I could not have been more pleased!

The next time we saw Megan, she was doing an event at the local Chick-fil-A where she worked. Jeff and I spotted her standing outside the restaurant. It was 50s theme day, and she was dressed up like she'd stepped off a movie set. She wore a large poodle skirt, saddle shoes, bright red lipstick, and her red hair styled perfectly to fit the occasion. Standing next to her was a tall man also dressed in 50s attire. It was Bob, her dad. It would not take us long to figure out how much she adored her father. They both greeted us with a hug like they've known us forever! Just like with my first son, I saw Mo with that proud look. I knew my boy had fallen in love.

It was the following spring, about a year after they dated, when Morgan told us he was going to ask Meg to marry him. Jeff, Jordan, and I along with her brother Jacob planned to meet that evening at her parent's, Bob and Denise's, home while Morgan took Megan to a restaurant. After dinner, they went for a walk where he proposed! When they arrived at the house, Megan came squealing through the front door, right into her mother's arms.

Deciding on a wedding date became challenging and emotional for Mo and Meg since Oryan was going to be deployed in a few months and they knew it wasn't going to be possible for him to be part of their wedding. I wondered how was I going to adjust to another deployment, which was approaching quickly, and my other sons' wedding without his brother. It was at that time my friend Pam, who also has three sons, gave me a poem from an unknown author titled "The Second Row." One of the stanzas read, "Then he met another that set his heart aglow. And I left my place of honor for a seat in the second row." This created an image for me of stepping back and letting go of what I could not control. It didn't mean the situation hurt less, but I did know that they tried their best when picking a wedding date and location.

Throughout the next few months, I noticed that Nan's shoes were starting to feel uncomfortable with each new step I took on my path of becoming a mother-in-law to another daughter. Just like having multiple children, you can't compare one with the other. I was already seeing the differences in my two daughters-in-law yet also seeing how they fit with each son.

It was wedding time, and I offered to help in hopes of hearing more of the little details of the wedding like what colors were being used, her dress design, flower selections, and the reception menu. I prayerfully waited while starting to plan the rehearsal dinner. On the big day, I saw that the girls wore dark blue, Megan's dress was gorgeous, the flowers were beautiful, and the food was delicious!

The wedding took place on a hot and cloudy July day, inside a barn a couple of hours away in the country. The setting was beautiful. The ceremony started with laughter as the flower girl and ring bearer came riding down the wood chip aisle in a child's black four-wheel-drive truck. Soon, the laughter turned into sniffles as we noticed the tears running down Morgan's cheeks when he saw Megan come down the aisle with her dad, who also had a tear-stained face! Brian had Mo and Meg start their lives together by serving one another. Mo took off his shoes and helped Meg remove her boots, and they washed each other's feet. At the same time, Brian explained the significance behind the story of how and why Jesus washed His disciples' feet (John 13: 1-17).

Later, he mentioned Oryan and his service to our country and how missing family events was one of the sacrifices placed on Military families. Danielle stood proud with the other brides-maids in her cowboy boots, tears rolling down her face and a hand on her baby bump. My mother's heart was truly full throughout the rest of the day. I felt at peace.

Soon, everyone was laughing again, although I can't recall why. I do remember that it was a great ceremony, not a dry eye in the barn! The reception was a blast and a six-foot cardboard cutout image of Oryan stood next to a canoe filled with beer! Those who knew him walked by and said, "Hi O!"

Everyone, including M&M (Mo and Meg), danced throughout the evening. Once the clock struck 10 pm sharp, they went running outside through a line of sparklers being waved by their friends and family. After the traditional tip the bride back kiss, they headed off into the night, driving a borrowed white four-wheel-drive truck!

Bob, Denise, Jeff, and I sat for a while longer, soaking in the memory of the evening. We knew how fortunate we were that M&M found each other. We talked about our grandchildren, who were just a thought at the time. Soon we found ourselves laughing at the possible adventures M&M would have as a married couple because of their personalities, not to mention once they start having children. And we were right. Megan says, "There's never a dull moment with Mo!" Jeff and I smile, knowing there's never a dull moment with Mo and Meg, and we love it!

Megan and my relationship came with its own challenges at times, due to our natures and lifestyles. Through trial and error, one thing has always been consistent, our desire to solve the conflict right then and there while the frustration and miscommunication are occurring — usually about little things like planning or how something was said. But addressing these concerns earlier than later alleviates the frustration and prevents it from turning into a big thing.

Megan and I, along with my granddaughters Avery and Rowan, recently took a five-hour car ride together on a family trip to Charleston. We went a day earlier than the guys, since they were still working. Although with small children, a long ride turns into more of an adventure, especially when potty training, it was fun being with her and my granddaughters. It's something we don't get to do very often. There wasn't a lack of conversation and our quiet moments were comfortable. She graciously listened as I read parts of this book to her while she drove my "grocery getter" van. As she laughed at some of the stories and shed tears at times, it was reassuring knowing that Meg connected to what was being said. She was actually sharing a piece of her heart. But what I really enjoyed was watching Meg drive a van!

I'm proud of this woman who put her career on hold to be available to her husband as he built his own career. She has done a great job pouring herself into raising her children and making a small two-bedroom house their home.

Nicki

Three years later, we had another wedding. I can't say that Nicki came into our lives as a stranger, because she did not. We have watched her grow up throughout the years along with Jordan's other friends at church. There was a group of them that met when they were about eight years old in Sunday school. They stayed in that group throughout high school, and most of them still keep in touch to this day.

Nicki always stood out to me, mostly due to her height and how she moved gracefully. At the time, she seemed soft-spoken, yet I have come to learn that being quiet doesn't always mean a person is timid. I'll elaborate more on that later.

Nicki's mom, Christy, and I were friends through the church, even before I knew her daughter. Because of that friendship, I found myself keeping an extra eye on Nicki during youth trips that her parents weren't on when she was younger. I always found comfort when it was the other way around. Knowing Christy was there eased my mind. Later, Christy and I realized our kids liked each other, yet they were trying to figure it out. We knew not to say a word! Actually, we were afraid that talking about them would jinx it, but in reality, we knew if it was God's plan, they would be together. Although, we still didn't allow ourselves to discuss it...in detail anyway!

During Jordan's High School years, I didn't realize he had feelings for Nicki, which he himself, could not explain when they were younger. To give you a little idea about my third daughter-in-law, I'll use the description Jordan wrote about her after their wedding, while I was putting together a scrapbook, she asked me to make with their photos. Here's a little of what he wrote:

"I always found Nicki to be very different from everyone else. The thing that stood out the most was her shoes. They were always really funky. And not the trend- setting kind of funky, but the funky that would have me questioning everything I knew about colors and matching. It was great! Then high school came around, and I no longer saw her by the shoes she wore, but rather by the person she was. She was still different in every way, but that's what was so attractive... and intimidating at the same time. It was an interesting feeling for sure. I fell in love with Nicki five years before we got married. Once she finally gave me a chance, it didn't take long to know she was the one."

As they dated in the months to follow, Nicki started spending more time at our home. Getting to know her in this way was different than at church with the other kids around. Come to find out, she was thrifty, organized and enjoyed working on crafts, then giving them away to other people. I noticed that although she was soft-spoken, she carried a sense of determination and confidence about herself. An example of this is the large arrow tattoo she had put across the top of her foot with the name, date of birth, and death of her best friend Alex. She passed away from complications of Crohn's disease the year before. The tattoo looks different to me now, for once I got to know Nicki better it all made sense. I see it now as an expression of her love for a friend, whom she misses dearly.

Seeing Jordan so relaxed around Nicki made Jeff and I feel relieved knowing he found someone laid back like himself. He's always been quieter than his two brothers and is never in a hurry. He's a hard worker and would stop to help anyone, just like Oryan and Morgan. One evening, Jordan sat with Jeff and I. He told us that he wanted to marry Nicki. He was finishing up school and had just started a new job in the city while still living at home. So as parents, we were a little concerned about the timing, but we knew that it was his decision to make. Knowing Christy and Steve (Nicki's dad), I was certain they would have the same concerns. They did, yet Jordan moved forward, bought a ring, and planned for the day he would ask Nicki to marry him. Our boy was in love.

Within weeks, we found ourselves gathering at her parents' home. Mo, Meg, John (Nicki's brother), Heather (Nicki's sister-in-law), Jeff, and I huddled in their den so we could hear Nicki and Jordan as they came through the door. When they arrived, it looked like they had been hiking with her dog, which is exactly what they had been doing! He took her hiking to one of their favorite Water Falls in North Georgia and proposed. Then ran almost the whole way back to the car! We all listened to the story of the proposal and congratulated them. The wedding planning began! It was a short, four-month engagement just like the other two brothers.

Nicki would carry her wedding planner everywhere she went over the next few months. While sitting at my kitchen table, I saw how the wedding was going to unfold. I rode along to sample the reception food and see the venue a few hours away in the mountains. I popped into the bridal shop to see her try on veils and met her bridesmaids. In the end, Christy decided to make the veil instead which turned out beautiful.

Nicki wore a wedding gown that Alex picked out to wear one day at her own wedding. Nicki wore it proudly on her own wedding day. Jordan and his brothers hung out the night before, which may have not been the best idea. When Jordan took his shirt off to shower in our hotel room while getting ready for the ceremony, I saw that his back was written all over with a black permanent marker! Normally, I would have chased the older boys around to put a good smack on their head (sorry, boy mom response), but I noticed that they were already getting paid back with a little headache of their own!

Just like with the other two weddings, Brian performed the ceremony. It was memorable to say the least. This time when the families all came up to pray together, each of my boys was there huddled around their brother lifting him and Nicki up in prayer.

The reception was a lot of fun, and the BBQ truly had a southern flavor! Alex's father John made cakes that were unique. The grooms' cake was like a mud pit that had a big blue lifted truck that actually spun out chocolate frosting-dirt onto the white wedding cake with chocolate-dipped strawberries! We danced until it was time to send Jordan and Nicki off. All the guests were lined up and rang little bells as Jordan and Nicki ran out to her black Chevy truck, she called Gibbs. And off they went!

After the kids pulled away, it was clean up time! The venue only provided the space, so wedding decor and food needed to be packed up. Plus, the whole floor had to be swept clean. As close friends and family worked together to be out of the venue within an hour, the owner came up and asked Christy and I how we knew each other? While we held onto our brooms, we told him that we were friends and I was the mother- in-law to her daughter. He paused and said he had never seen this before. I asked what this was. He proceeded to say, "I've never seen the groom's parents stay to help clean up. It's nice to see." Christy and I thanked him for the compliment, knowing we wouldn't have done it any other way.

I can't recall Nicki and I ever being frustrated with each other. Maybe it's our personalities or that we both had the advantage of being around each other on and off throughout the years. Plus, our families already knew each other through church. Although there will most likely come a time when we're faced with obstacles, I'd like to think that my time as a mother-in-law to Danielle and Megan has taught me how to communicate more effectively. Not perfect, just better.

Nicki is quiet yet smart and strong. She's flexible with change, for who else can live in a house with a kitchen under construction for eight months after coming home with a new baby? She did and made it work. She made it home.

As you have heard, what I started off expecting as a mother-in-law is not how it unfolded. In my mind, I thought the girls would love me from the moment we met, but in reality, what relationship starts off that way? It took time just like it will take you time to get to know the woman who captured your son's heart. I wish Nan could have met each one of my daughters-in-law. She would have grown to love them all—and like me, they would have loved Nan.

These days, Nans shoes aren't feeling as snug. I guess they have been broken in with each daughter that I have been blessed to call my own. They are wonderful mothers to Jeff's and my grandchildren, which includes the three granddaughters mentioned earlier. Jordan and Nicki's two boys, Griffin and Barrett along with another granddaughter on the way.

A realization: I do know that all three of these strong women and myself started off with something in common. We came into this family the same way—our love for the boys.

9

Her Mom

To not mention the boy's mother-in law would make this book feel incomplete. After speaking to women who have a son-in-law, the topic isn't usually as sensitive due to the fact her daughter seems more comfortable with her own mother and the guy seems to go with the flow of the schedule his wife lays out. She can speak freely with her own mom or even argue without the long-term consequences of hurt feelings, which can occur with the mother-in-law. Mothers and daughters seem to rebound faster from their different opinions. Words aren't replayed as if they were set in stone unlike with the mother-in-law where the new wife may feel like she's being judged. The son-in-law, in most cases, is accommodating to his mother-in-law maybe because he knows that there's going to be good food during the visit or, most likely, he knows his wife doesn't feel as tense. This goes back to the mother-in-law and daughter-in-law seeing and hearing differently.

Working in a profession that cares for women, I have heard and seen some funny moments when a mother-in-law and son-in-law are in the same room. When the girl's mother comes with her daughter for an obstetric visit, she comes into the room beaming with the anticipation of being able to see an ultrasound or hear the heartbeat of her grandchild. I usually like to watch the guy's expression when I ask about his mom in a general way. The anticipation of becoming a grandmother can be such a special time for both women.

"Do both moms live nearby?" He usually turns his head to look at the wife before he answers, not quite sure what to say about this subject.

Even before I started writing on this subject or having grand-children of my own, this always seemed like an exciting time for everyone to share or at least given the option to be included.

I'm happy to say that each of my boys actually cares for his mother-in-law and over the years has grown to love her. My boys speak of them highly. Although I'm sure they see the differences in each of us as mothers.

My daughters-in-law are fortunate to have grown up with strong mother figures. Each of them is a conscientious and caring young women, which is a reflection of how they were raised.

Their mothers Kathy, Denise, and Christy are ladies who I now call my friends due to the fact that we have been able to share in many life events as mothers. We enjoy the moments we can gather together as an extended family, especially during the births of our grandchildren, working alongside each other as grandparents to help bring relief to our adult children and their busy schedules. I understand that this isn't an option in some families due to various reasons, but it is an effort worth making if possible. It will hope-fully give the grandchildren a healthy memory of their whole family being together.

For my sons, having a mother-in-law has been a good oppor-tunity for them to see how girls are usually raised differently than boys—even if there are boys and girls in the same household. The tone of how subjects are approached is different with girls than with boys. When I was an elementary school nurse for two years, I would unintentionally make the girls cry due to the way I would say something to them. Yet the same thing could be said to the boys in the exact same tone, and their responses would be totally different. Over time, I learned to watch my words and my tone with the girls. Soon, they were stopping by to see me for what I called a "happy hug" during the day when they passed by the clinic. Now when the boys, who are my comfort zone, would pop in, I'd say, "Why are you here again?" Their grinning response was usually, "Awe, Ms. Cathy, can I have a cough drop?" Of course, they came by for food! The older boys got a cough drop and a sample of deodorant for obvious reasons! Again, I heard, "Awe, Ms. Cathy!"

As parents age, it can be challenging to be patient. At times, I've noticed that a son-in-law often responds with a gentler tone to his mother-in-law than even her own daughter. I say that from my own personal experience and observations by watching Jeff with my parents over the years. These moments haven't gone unnoticed. You would assume that this is one of those little things, but it's a big thing for me.

As a mother of boys, I find myself trying to create time with my boys or call them just to hear their voices and to learn what they have been up to. Whereas, being a mother of a daughter, you may find that you are sharing time with her husband— wanting moments to go shopping, eat lunch together, or chat on the phone. Certainly, being a mother-in-law to the man who loves your daughter can bring its own challenges of adjusting your usual time spent with each other.

Once we become a mother-in-law to the boy or girl, it's like gaining another adult child. The image we portray is up to us.

10

Creating Memories

Like most parents, our children consumed the majority of our time and thoughts throughout the years. Although there were different stages during their childhood and teenage years that required even more energy, ultimately their success and happiness were our priority. Hopefully, the force that drives parents is love. It surely drove us to be active in our childrens' lives. We didn't want to miss anything because we enjoyed spending time with our boys. I still think to this day that we all grew and learned from each other along the way.

Sometimes, when we are all together, an old memory will surface of an event, situation, or even a whooping they received as a child. It's interesting how everyone has an interpretation of the way they remember the details. We each tell a different story, even though we were all in the same place at the same time. In the end, we are usually laughing about how we all saw the memory from a different perspective, especially when talking about a whooping they received due to something they did or said that was disrespectful! I guess you can call it a comparison to the behavior of adults. What we say and do without respecting others usually ends up with consequences. It may not be a whooping, but someone will feel the sting.

Each family has a different way of communicating love. The dynamics are unique with distinct traditions and habits that seem normal and fun to each family. The size of a family also plays a role. To think about combining or extending families could be potentially complicated and, in some cases, not well received, especially if the families have different values. Your impression and personal expectations of this new family can go either way. This is also true of grandparenting.

During our boy's childhood years, Jeff and I made an effort for the boys to have a relationship with their grandparents on both sides. Although we fussed at the spoiling of extra treats, they now have memories to share with their children and grandchildren.

My boys will remember picking blueberries in Grandpa's garden and riding on his lawnmower, swimming and jumping off the diving board. They'll remember enjoying Grandma's desserts and driving with her in the big blue Cadillac. Running and playing with the neighbor boys, Kyle and Kody, was O and Mo's favorite thing to do!

They'll remember eating on TV trays at Nanny and Pawpaw's house. Camping and bonfires. Walking to the barn for a huggie drink (a fruit drink in a barrel-shaped plastic container) in their underwear and rainboots. I'm sure they can still hear Nanny say, "Make the cow happy!" Then get praised for finishing their milk! Of course, the memory of "Mary White's Party" too—a make-believe party she would take them to as they closed their eyes to go to sleep. Oh yes, Jordan will remember, ice cream in bed as a treat!

How easily we could have let our parenting differences interfere with the creation of memories that allowed our children to feel a grandparents' love. This is another example of how God doesn't waste anything. He's constantly teaching. Jeff and I didn't have the convenience of grandparents living locally during our own childhoods. Yet instead of feeling deprived due to circumstances out of our control, we felt a desire to make these memories possible for our children.

Now as a grandparent myself, I am grateful to see that time and technology have changed to allow long-distance grandparenting to be possible. Through Facetime, I cherish reading stories and listening to my grandchildren tell me about their days. I can even participate in bath time while staying dry! But this is only possible because my daughters-in-law (and sons) take the time to include me and Jeff. In return, we take the time to be included.

Our grandchildren call Jeff Bubba, named after his own maternal grandfather. If you saw both of their tidy garages, you would have seen that this was a perfect name for him. They call me Boppi, a shortened version of Bebop (the name my daughters-in- law gave me). My first granddaughter couldn't pronounce Bebop. It came out sounding like Boppi. Of course, whatever name the grandchild called me was going to stick! So now, even my daughters-in-law call me Boppi with an occasional Bebop thrown in there at times when they see me busy.

It's common for a girl to call her mom and share in the little events throughout the day since this is what most mothers and daughters do. Yet through time and having children of their own, I feel that my daughters-in-law have been considerate of my longing to be part of the little things too. Boy or girl mom, we love the same! To be part of our children and grandchildren's lives brings us joy. Most of the time, that means getting in the car and heading down the road to where they live to be part of an activity or to babysit so our adult children can have a night out. Of course, there are those times when the little cherubs come to Bubba and Boppi's house! I actually like to call it a physical fitness time with hugs and kisses.

As I watch my own grandchildren play together, I know the effort that goes into giving them this time, which brings so much joy to them and to me and Jeff. These little children remind me of the meals Nan put together during the holidays and of all the gifts she wrapped. They remind me of the Easter egg hunts she made possible. I can still see her five grandsons and one grand-daughter running around, looking for the hidden eggs around the yard or climbing on the squeaky metal swing set. One of the best memories is everyone playing and hanging out in the backyard, swimming or floating in the above ground pool. Often, you would see Pawpaw taking his afternoon nap, swaying in the hammock under the big shade tree. Lunch would be served on the small back porch, which got a fresh coat of red paint each summer. The kids would sit at the table while the adults leaned or sat on the railing. Even with the grill radiating heat and the sun beating down on the porch, everyone managed to cram on it together and eat.

Mealtime is always a way to bring people together. It's tastier when my daughters-in-law bring a new recipe they cooked or even a stop at the store for a side dish or dessert. It's one less thing I need to prepare. It allows me time to sit and enjoy everyone's company too. You will always find a stack of paper plates and cups at my house, because I don't want to clean up either! Oh, the joys of getting older and letting go!

Looking back, I very seldom brought a prepared dish to Nan's home, which I now see would have brought her relief from so much food preparation. It was so simple, yet I never thought to pick up the phone to coordinate a menu with my sisters-in-law or even ask Nan, "What can I bring?" Eek, I certainly failed in that area! But knowing her, she would have said, "I already have it all."

But I do remember helping Nan dry dishes since there wasn't a dishwasher in her 1960s kitchen, which still had old white metal cabinets and Formica countertops. Nor did she have any other luxuries that were found in the more modern 1980s kitchens. Here's a scary memory. I can still see her lighting a match and holding it under the burner to start the stove! Yet as I mentioned earlier, she was simple, and it was peaceful in her home.

11

All in a Day's Work

Once I committed to writing about the relationship between mothers-in-law and daughters-in-law, I was more in tuned to this subject and the relationships around me, especially as an Obgyn nurse. I would hear subtle comments that were hurtful to both the daughter-in-law and mother-in-law at work and even in public. I never understood how we could throw out words in general conversations that could potentially hurt someone's feelings. It's likely that these words are felt more than heard. On occasions, I would inquire about a comment I may have heard about a daughter-in-law or mother-in-law. Having been on both sides, I feel for each woman. A few questions I briefly ask these days, depending on the conversation, are: What kind of daughter-in-law would you want? Are you the kind of daughter-in-law you would want to have one day? Are you the mother-in-law you would have wanted or had? For my pregnant patients having a boy, the most common response I hear is, "I never thought of it that way." It's a typical response once the realization occurs that she will be walking in her mother-in-law's shoes one day.

At times, I do hear, "My mother-in-law is wonderful" or "my daughter-in-law is awesome." Those words literally feel like a fresh breeze.

Not long ago, I had a patient close to delivering her third boy. As I was taking her blood pressure, I glanced at her two cute little boys sitting in the chair. I said to her, "You're going to have daughters-in-law one day." I mentioned to her that I have three daughters-in-law. We chatted briefly about the subject of being a mother-in-law. A few weeks later, she returned for one of her final appointments a bit frustrated with a recent encounter with her mother-in-law. She mentioned that she remembered our conversation and paused before responding to her mother-in-law, asking herself, "What kind of daughter-in-law do I want to have one day. How would I want her to respond to me?"

"How did that go?" I asked her. She said it was helpful and she felt better with the outcome of their conversation.

I went to see her in the hospital after she delivered her baby. As I walked into her room, she asked if I had passed her mother-in-law and boys in the hallway. I told her I didn't recall seeing them, but I was glad she was able to come help and enjoy this special time.

Working in a profession that takes care of women brings a lot of challenges. Patients come to us during their pregnancies and most of the time it goes well. Yet there are those occasions of loss. There are healthy women exams. You can call them "maintenance check-ups," which are usually routine. Then there are those in pain, not just physically due to an illness but emotionally due to life situations that are out of their control. I see how my career has shaped me, and I'm grateful for the patients I have served and the people I have worked alongside over all these years in Georgia and in Virginia. Some of them have become my dearest friends whom I have treasured for many years.

12

Different Paths

At this point, you may be saying, "But you don't understand my situation! You don't understand my mother-in-law (or daughter-in-law)." You're absolutely right! But I must ask, do you know this other woman? Have you actually taken the time to sit a moment, to try to understand or learn about her? I don't know what kind of heart each mother-in-law and daughter-in-law has, yet I do know there's no way of understanding each other without investing a little time in one another. It is an investment, with a potentially big return.

Not every daughter-in-law was raised the same. Some may have challenges or hidden hurts. Some may be healthy and happy. Some may not have had a loving mother. Some may not have a mother in their lives at all. Some may feel entitled. Some may have no faith, while others walk in their faith. Some may have had a great childhood and role models. Some may have been abused emotionally, physically, or verbally. Some may find this information enlightening, yet there are those who may not connect with this book at all. Some may not even want to try because too much time has passed and the relationship appears irreparable. Although, some may take the first step to forgive and start over.

In the same regards, not every mother-in-law was raised the same. Some may have had challenges or hidden hurts. Some may feel entitled. Some may be healthy and happy. Some may have no faith, while others walk in their faith. Some may have been abused emotionally, physically, or verbally. Some may have led a great life raising their families while some may be tired, weary, or lonely. Some may find this information enlightening, and there are those who may not connect to this book at all. Some may not even want to try because too much time has passed and the relationship appears irreparable. Although, some may take the first step to forgive and start over.

Looking back, I probably would have thought: What is the big deal about these relationships? Now, I would say, women are a big deal! Young, middle-aged, or older, we are all women of influence. We need our coffee time, sit on the bed or a bench time, take a walk time, just a moment of time to get to know each other. I'm not talking about being best friends but simply being able to respect each other, knowing where we each have been and where we are in life today.

Of course, there are those situations where the relationship is actually unhealthy or toxic, and it's certainly understandable to not put yourself around a person who can be draining. But to invest a few moments of time can still be beneficial to form your own opinion. You may see or hear that person differently than someone else's description of who she is and her problems.

We aren't here to fix or change people, and most importantly, we're not to judge one another. Through time, I've learned that accepting and loving people right where they are maybe the only Jesus they see or feel in the middle of their personal struggles or addictions. How they perceive our presence is up to them, for in the end, we are only responsible for how we treat others. Some people are just unhappy human beings for whatever reason. It's okay to not get anything back for your time, and you may even find that you're criticized for putting in the effort.

13

The Girls Tell Their Stories

Danielle

I call her Boppi. The first time I saw her was in a photograph I saw in September my junior year in College. Oryan had a picture of his family sitting on the lawn in front of their cute gray house. My initial thoughts were joy-filled and a deep yearning to be part of his family. His mom looked energetic, fun, and happy. I finally got to meet Oryan's parents in October of our senior year. My suspicions of my mother-in-law were true; she was fun, energetic, and not to mention young! After introductions, we ventured out into the city for dinner. I was so excited to meet Cathy and get to know her and Jeff.

As November and December came, Oryan and I began to make holiday plans. I was able to spend some time visiting the Lopes' home before Thanksgiving. I walked into their ranch-style home and was greeted by his parents and younger brother. Their house smelled like sweet buttercream and the tones of reds and browns enveloped me in a warm hug. We sat and talked for what seemed like hours, which gave me a small glimpse of what family meant to them. As Christmas neared, we wanted to be together, so I invited Oryan to New Jersey to spend Christmas with my family. Looking back, I realize my mother-in-law had to make a hard decision to allow Oryan to come spend his first Christmas away from home with us or keep him in Georgia. I'm so grateful for this now because I know she could have demanded and ensured one more Christmas home together before the military began dictating when and where Christmas' would be in the future.

As the new year progressed, we became engaged and started planning our wedding. I knew I not only wanted my mother heavily involved but also my future mother-in-law. I got ready at my parent's house and invited her to come and join us. We sat eating, laughing, and enjoying the festivities between hair and make-up. I think I remember Cathy asking if someone could style her hair after doing my mom's and grandmother's hair. You might think I was (am) crazy for offering, but I was glad to include her in the fun and giddiness that spread throughout the house as we sprayed, curled, and pinned.

After the wedding, a few years had passed, and we were about to have a baby. When I had our daughter, Oryan was deployed, and I was hundreds of miles from my family. I invited both sets of parents to come be there when the baby was born. I had friends and other women advise me against this, but I knew in my heart that I wanted to share this moment with them. After I gave birth, the doctor could not stop the bleeding. I was medevaced to another hospital to receive care, and my newborn baby was left behind. Thankfully I had two sets of parents to step in and care for my child. This event was a turning point for our two families and brought us closer together.

As I spent more time with the Lopes family, I began to notice I was frustrated, annoyed, and angry towards my mother-in-law. I didn't want this and searched for methods to stop acting this way, but the reality of my sin was deep. I was so unhappy and knew I could not continue feeling this disconnect between us, so I sought an older, wiser woman in my church to counsel me biblically. Her advice came from Mark 12:30- 31, NIV: "And you should love the Lord your God...and love your neighbor as yourself." She advised me to love and serve Cathy more than myself. This was so hard, but as I dealt with my sin, Cathy was patient, slow to anger, kind, and loving. As I continue to truly get to know my mother-in-law as well as my own mother, I am blessed by them greatly.

Growing up, I played the big sister role well. I was protective and motherly, but my sister didn't need another mother. She needed a best friend. However, there was a turning point in our relationship when I stopped acting like a mom and started acting like a friend. She has seen me at my best, my worst, know my faults, and my strengths. I don't have to explain my intentions or my idiosyncrasies; she already knows them. I had similar expectations of sisters-in-law, mostly from observation of my family. I know how my sister handles and perceives things, but I was just gifted two sisters-in-law who I need to be patient with and figure things out as we go. I try to love them the best I can with God's help. Gaining two sisters-in-law later in life was a true joy.

Megan

The moments and experiences I have had over the last decade have been a huge part of shaping me into the daughter-in-law I am today. Attempting to sum everything up into a coherent narrative seems overwhelming. After a recent road trip, Cathy began sharing her heart and passion behind this book. When she asked me to contribute, I wasn't quite sure how to articulate our transformation into a few quotes or soundbites. Being vulnerable is a struggle, especially when there are topics and struggles, we are still learning to work through. Cheers, Boppi!

I can't quite remember what life was like before calling the Lopes family my own. It has been eight years since I married the middle son, Morgan. I call him Mo. At the time, he was my knight in shining armor. (He was a cast member at Medieval Times.) He was working his way through college with three jobs. I quickly fell in love with his passion for life. Before we started dating, I attended church with him one Sunday morning and began to see the impact his parents had on shaping his character. I remember meeting Cathy, Mo's mom. Even then, she was a beautiful woman. She had a tender spirit and a kind smile. She wrapped her arms around Mo the moment she saw him and introduced herself and

Jeff. I did not know it then but soon discovered what an honor and a joy it was to be a Lopes girl.

Morgan and I dated for a little less than a year. We got engaged then married in the summer of 2012. We spent many days in our families' homes leading up to the wedding. It was something that was important to us. His parent's place was always warm. A candle seemed to always be burning. It was strikingly clean and welcoming. If Cathy knew Morgan was coming over, there would be warm brownies in the oven. Despite Mo being one of the healthiest humans I know, he would never turn down one of his mom's brownies. This is still true today.

In an instant, the act of saying "I do" means you gain a new family and new loved ones. In my situation, I gained two brothers and two sisters-in-law. There is also a growing crew of nieces and nephews. We are each very unique. Everyone has different passions in life but one thing I know about everyone is how much we each love our families fiercely.

Cathy, Danielle, Nicki, and I are all 'Lopes girls'. It has taken time to find our groove and to learn how to communicate effectively. It has not been perfect. There are tensions when communicating, around holidays, throughout planning logistics, etc. But it is a process we continue to work through. We plan differently, think differently, and communicate differently as well. I like things written down and being specific. In getting to know Cathy, she likes to talk things through or plan collaboratively. It has taken time for me to be comfortable with the fact that we process things in our own way. Neither is right nor wrong. Neither good nor bad. Our approaches are just different.

When coming together for major milestones, holidays, or life events, I have learned that we are all working toward the same goal. We want time together and new memories to share. Strong bonds take time to develop. Be patient, be gracious, and be open to imperfection.

Nicki

My name is Nicki, and I am married to Jeff and Cathy's youngest son, Jordan. My family attended the same church as the Lopes growing up, and I have known Jordan since we were about eight years old. We started off in the same class at church, which later morphed into friendship in high school, and we had mini crushes on and off until we finally decided to date after college, getting married a short nine months later once we realized how it was meant to be. In middle school and high school, I was used to having Cathy around in the youth group at church. One of my first memories of interacting with Cathy was on a youth retreat. A group of us were walking along a path by the lake and Cathy asked me to stop and take her and "JoJo's" picture. Little did she know then that my picture taking abilities left some room for improvement. (Luckily DIL number one is a great photographer). I remember how she and Jordan teased me after they saw how off-center the photos were. After that, she was always in my life as my friend, Jordan's mom. Cathy always seemed so put together in all areas of life (and still does). She always dressed fashionably, had three good looking boys, volunteered in the youth group, had a full-time job, and kept an exceptionally clean house. When I was younger, I didn't think much of it except for thinking it was pretty impressive.

Then, I started dating Jordan. It went from being impressive to intimidating. How would I compete as the main woman in Jordan's life when he was used to perfection from his mom? In the few months of Jordan and I dating and being engaged, Cathy and I spent a lot of time with each other, and I really got to know her more. While yes, she is very put together, I now know her as Cathy, the person and mother rather than the perfect mom of my friend. I understand her more. I see that she gets so much accomplished because she never sits still! I see that she loves her three boys with all of her heart and does all that she can to make their lives all they can be. I see her giving heart and am learning more and more about what shaped her spirit to give as she was growing up and became a daughter-in-law herself.

Jordan and I have been married for a few years now, but I have felt like part of the family since the beginning. Jeff and Cathy are both so loving and welcoming to me and my fellow sisters-in-law. I have not only gained a husband in my marriage but an extension of family that feels like my own. I have gained sisters who I never had growing up all so different from each other. It's hard to believe we all married into the same family.

Each of my sisters-in-law is so different. We have had to learn a lot about each other as we work to grow and raise our families. We all parent differently, live differently, even eat differently; yet we are all part of one family. And we make it work. It sometimes gets crazy and chaotic. It is sometimes so unplanned it boggles my mind. But we know without a doubt how much the others loves their husbands and how much our husbands love their brothers. So even when things get a little crazy, we have that strong love that brings it all together. Becoming a daughter-in-law has been different than I imagined, not harder or easier, just different. It has shown me how to grow and adapt to new family habits while learning to create our own within our marriage. It has shown me how to come into a family that was not my own yet wholeheartedly become a part of that family. And through it all, would you believe Cathy still asks me to take the pictures?

My Sister-in-Law

I found it important to include my own sister-in-law Brenda in this part of the book since she has a story and advise some young women may be able relate to. I enjoy watching her lovingly raise two sons while juggling her family activities and career as a middle-aged woman. She easily could have grown bitter and resentful of the life she did not have as a child. For all of us, she has a way of making sure everyone's birthdays are special, since she knows what it feels like to grow up without a party or be celebrated. Brenda and my mom have developed a unique relationship over the years. It's through that time she went from being my brother's wife to also becoming my mother's third daughter.

Brenda

"My situation in life was different as I did not have a mom. My parents divorced when I was a baby, and my grandparents raised me, which was a blessing in its own right. When I met my mother-in-law Ellie and married into the family, my feelings were one of inclusiveness from the start. I now had this woman in my life who was like a mom to me, a supportive friend and confidant, all of which I did not need in my life but desired unbeknownst to me. She embraced me with open arms and was always there, no matter what the circumstances and without judgement. I didn't have any expectations around her or her intentions other than she was always warm, kind, and generous.

I never looked at her in any other way than as my mom, that truly filled a void inside me even if I didn't know it at the time. When you don't have a maternal person in your life, you can become hard, independent, and strong; but Ellie brought out all the positives. I know that I can always count on her to be there when needed without me even asking. She just stepped in to help with my growing family. Although some would call this intrusive, I called it unconditional love and didn't take it personally as that was not her heart.

Whether you have a mom, sister, aunt, or friend, you will always have room for all the women in your life, including your mother-in-law. Even when the situation isn't typical, it can be an amazing feeling to know you are blessed to have someone in your corner. I am forever grateful for this unconditional love."

With what you have heard these young women say, you may be able to plug-in your own stories of the women in your life.

Hopefully, your new relationships have been a positive experience. Or maybe like us, through all the good times, there is an occasional need for patience and seeing with new eyes. One day, you will look back and cry or maybe even laugh over the events that have led you to where you are today. The goal is to have a grateful heart and not grow bitter. To be able to step up, speak up, or step back.

As a mother-in-law, we come into this new relationship with more life experiences. Not knowing it all but simply living longer. Whether we have had good or bad life lessons, time has been our teacher and our healer. In that regard, if someone is going to step back and offer grace, it should be us first. I'm not saying this to make you feel like you are being walked over but to present yourself as being humble, giving yourself time to consider your responses so they are healthy and mature. Even though I'm saying this, it doesn't mean that I'm always able to follow through with my responses in this manner. On those occasions, I fall under the title of crazy woman! I'm certain we all have a little of that in us. Just saying.

In the book of Ruth, Naomi knew her role and refused to have Ruth follow her back to her hometown of Bethlehem. I'm sure Naomi would have appreciated the company but knew the road was going to be hard and not a safe journey for a young woman, never mind what she was going to face in her hometown once she returned. Naomi also wanted her daughter-in-law to be able to remarry and have a family of her own since she was a widow. She encouraged her to go home to her mother. But in the end, Ruth made her own decision to go with Naomi. When Naomi stepped back in her own desires, it gave Ruth a chance to step up. Ruth was able to encourage Naomi in her moments of anger, fear, and self-pity due to her circumstances. These women were able to survive by working together. Although their journey was tough along the way and the future at the time was uncertain, the ending was beautiful.

A story worth reading

14

Butterflies and Dreams

Over the twenty years following my mother-in-law's death, I would find myself remembering the woman I called Nan. I have mostly remembered when I see butterflies fluttering around. It reminds me of the day after she died when a yellow butterfly was literally around me all day. It was at my front door, near my car, and beside me when I walked into the store. At home, when I looked out my kitchen window, it was there again-a single yellow butterfly. Maybe it was the season for butterflies or maybe they have always been around, but that particular day, I noticed the yellow butterfly. It's a peaceful feeling that I still enjoy each time I see one.

I also remember Nan when my daughters-in-law are near me. The girls may not understand it now, but they bring me comfort and sweet memories of my time with Nan. Without realizing it back then, the memories I made are what I would pull from in the years to come.

Having a daughter was a new feeling for me. It has been a learning process, a time to slow down, to listen and speak with a different perspective. As I mentioned earlier, something I would normally blurt out to the boys, would not go over as well with the girls.

Prior to each of us developing a relationship, if I had said something that unintentionally hurt the girls' feelings, the boys would let me know. Ouch! My response to them would be, "That's not what I meant." Early on, I seldom received support from the guys since they were trying to protect their wives' feelings. I knew that they heard only one side of the conflict. I also understood that they were new husbands, which brings its own challenges. Although, it left me feeling hurt on occasions, like a child being reprimanded. It brought back a memory of when my father-in-law mentioned that Babe sometimes cried at night because her feelings were hurt. Here is another lesson about walking in someone else's shoes. The path isn't always paved, for there can be rugged terrain you have to get through without much assistance. That's when taking one step at a time pays off.

Here's where the tug of war could have started. At times, it can be exhausting for all of us, not knowing how and when to say something. Keep in mind I have three daughters-in-law, all with three unique personalities. All wonderful and strong women! Like me, they have an opinion and want to be heard. Yet they have gained only one mother-in-law to learn about. So, to say I'm a little outnumbered at times is an understatement. My resources were limited on how to handle these situations without reacting hastily. Here's where stepping back for a moment has its advantages. Ultimately, I knew I wanted to continue a strong relationship with my boys and be able to enjoy having daughters in my life.

I thought about the girlfriends I have and how each relationship is different and unique. Then it dawned on me; what I may say or do for one friend, may not be the same approach I chose for another friend. Once I started responding to each of my daughters- in-law individually, things improved. What I say and do for one daughter-in-law may not be the same way I approach the other two.

You may presume that this sounds like a lot of work. But once we actually got to know each other better, it made more sense, and it happens now without overthinking the outcome.

I have learned that Megan enjoys fresh cut flowers, so I wouldn't get her the same plant I would get Nicki who enjoys crafts and gardening. Danielle enjoys cooking from scratch, so when she is creating a dish, I help clean up, which offers us time together in the kitchen and keeps me from feeling frustrated over all the dishes. My other daughters-in-law would not choose to be in the kitchen as much—although we all enjoy the taste of Danielle's labor of love! So, if you ever come to my house when everyone is home, there will probably be some beautifully arranged fresh flowers from Megan, the smell of something cooking from Danielle, and a homemade craft of some sort from Nicki. It's nice that we can now all enjoy each other's gifts along the way.

My contribution is music! Yet, it doesn't take long before I hear one of the girls, or all of them, giggle and say, "What is she listening to?" Within minutes, the music is changed and cranked up louder! Here's where I can choose to be offended or choose to dance to their music! So, I choose to dance to their music and appreciate their different personalities. Nowadays, we enjoy creating memories of us all being together, along with a glass of wine or two and the music cranked up!

I hesitated to mention the dream I had a few short months after Nan passed away, but I feel it's an important example of how God reveals himself to us. It occurred around February 2000. The dream came with a veil of darkness, the blackest I've ever seen. It wasn't just dark from the beginning of the dream; it became darkness, if that makes sense. I remember commenting on the blackness after I woke up. Within the same thought of the darkness came a light appearing from the top left corner. The brightness came floating toward me. It didn't radiate light, but it was a glow. I didn't feel the need to squint, but it was as bright as the sun. As the light came closer, it gently opened up, and there was Nan. She was in the light. She was the light. I recall saying in a whisper, as if the air was seeping from my lungs, "Nan, you're so beautiful."

I became aware at that moment that this was not a dream. Her face was a glow of perfection, no wrinkles or suntan. Her body was not visible as she was surrounded in white, like a robe. The lack of knowing God's word, in this case, kept me from fully understanding what was taking place in what seemed like only a few moments. However, I did ask her, "How is it?"

She replied, "It's good. I'm on the other side now." Her expression wasn't full of joy, but there was calmness and peacefulness to her words. She mentioned her best friend Gayle by name, yet I cannot recall the exact conversation. Then the vision was over.

I woke up instantly knowing what just happened was real. I told Jeff in the morning that I saw his mom, and he said, "I wish I could have a dream of her." I told him that I didn't think it was a dream. I couldn't quite place my emotions or verbalize how it made me feel, but over the next few months, I started reading the Bible every day. I had a feeling that there was a connection between life and death, like there was more to see.

Throughout the years, bits and pieces of what I saw became clearer. Sometimes I would recognize a similarity in a message I heard in church or a verse I read in the Bible.

Even though I may have read that verse many times, I'm still amazed at how we can see and hear differently as we mature in our faith and spend time in God's word. Many years later, I learned that Gayle had spoken to her about salvation through Jesus Christ during their last visit together. Gayle said, "I told her, I'll see you in heaven, Babe".

15

Change of Seasons

After Nan died, I thought my role as a daughter-in-law was over. I was thirty- four years old and didn't know that I had much more to learn from the woman I called Nan. Remember, God doesn't waste any time on earth. It isn't Nan's words that I remember most but how she treated others. How she treated me when she didn't have to. How she was patient and kind when she probably didn't feel like it. How her body and mind could be struggling at the change of seasons in her life and in her body. I didn't know to pay attention to her occasional remarks that were out of character for her, although I easily could have been offended. Only recently have I been able to experience this new realization since I am now experiencing the M word—menopause! This stage of life makes PMS (premenstrual syndrome) look like a piece of cake! The symptoms aren't just a few days out of the month. They are the whole month and the years to follow. Ice water has become my new best friend! It really does help!

Even as I write these words, I am faced with my own struggles, acknowledging personal feelings that have surfaced throughout this process while all along trying to be a good example to my sons and daughters-in-law. In reality I'm tired. I want to cry constantly, and at times, the feeling of wanting to walk away from everything sounds appealing. Then those feelings make me sound and feel ungrateful. They also contradict the love I have for my family. So, I cry again and pray for peace. I pray for a pure heart and mind.

I pray that the fruit of the Spirit resonates in all I say and do (Galatians 5:22) and throughout these pages. In prayer, it's obvious that God is in control. In prayer, we are reminded that He loves us. In prayer, we can let go and let God direct our steps by seeking His kingdom first (Matthew 6:22), knowing His plan is perfect and timely.

Writing this book has allowed me to understand myself better, not just the roles I have in life but how God designed me. I better understand how to use the gifts that I have been given—gifts that I thought were just something I enjoyed doing without realizing they are intended to glorify Him by sharing with others. With that realization also comes Satan, who has tried to derail this book from being shared in various ways these last few months. Through these times, God has placed unlikely friendships in my path to strengthen me and even expose emotions that were tucked away deep inside. One of the advantages of carrying scripture in your heart is that when your mind starts telling you one thing, God's word speaks louder!

I actually had no intention of elaborating on this season of life. Yet once I started typing, it occurred to me that if you aren't going through it now, one day you will. At this point, you can plug-in you're version of this season. Either you're the mother-in-law going through menopause or you're the daughter-in-law, and it's a great time to extend grace when needed. Sort of like paying it forward.

Again, growing older has advantages. It gives us an opportunity to see how the past has directed our lives, how even some of the bad times may have turned into something positive (Romans 8:28). For my family, moving to Georgia after Nan passed away was a huge blessing for us all. We probably would not have moved when the opportunity arose if she had still been living. As the years continue to pass, it has become more evident that this is where God wanted us to grow our family. I see this clearly now through each of my daughters-in-law and the people we have met through our church, school, and work over the years. It reminds me that there is a time and season for everything.

16

Little Things

Like in a movie and in life, you can see how someone can allow themselves to become bitter or resentful over decisions they've made or dreams that didn't come true. Sometimes loneliness is a person's biggest enemy. You can also see how a person has grown within a lifetime, by overcoming challenges or becoming the best friend, wife, and mother she can be despite the obstacles.

I cannot leave out the women who don't have children of their own or those who have yet to get married and start their family. Throughout the years, I have watched these friends care for and love on my boys. These same women have also nurtured, loved, and comforted me along the way. It's the little things, like being an extra hand on a busy day at home or at work, offering an ear to listen or a shoulder to cry on when needed. More than likely, we can all place a name to these women in our lives. They can be like a breath of fresh air for us, and they don't even realize what they have done. Relief can come by doing the little things for one another, for we never really know what someone else is going through.

We are all women just doing life and can always use an extra person to count on. If you invest time in others, which involves being more than a casual friend, you will develop these dear friends along the way. If you don't have these kinds of friends, then you can always be one.

For me, welcoming a new neighbor one spring day turned into a unique friendship that I will always hold dear in my heart.

This friendship started when I welcomed my new neighbor with fresh cookies. Lin opened the front door with the warmest smile and invited me in to have a glass of wine. I'm certain there were other things I probably felt I should have been doing in the middle of the day, yet I agreed. I sat on a barstool at the counter and chatted awhile. We laughed about simple things and briefly talked about ourselves and our families.

I asked what brought her to Georgia and what made her want to buy a big home for just herself? (By that time, we were on our second glass of wine). She responded that she had stage IV recurrent breast cancer and wanted to be closer to her grandchildren and her family. Wow, I would have loved to have seen the expression on my face as I looked around at all the unpacked boxes then back at my new friend in her mid-sixties. She was smiling, probably knowing she caught me off guard.

Within two years, the cancer started taking over her body. I found myself helping with little things that would save her energy. Another neighbor would bring her mail to the porch where a full-size mailbox was placed so Lin didn't have to walk up the driveway. Jeff started taking out her trash and bringing in her trash can from the street. Soon, the grass began to wear down between our homes as I ran back and forth a number of times during the day and night to help with her personal and medical needs.

I quickly learned that this lady was strong-willed in many areas, which included the relationships in her life. But being a fairly new friend, my role was different. I valued what I became to her in those last months of her life. I saw that she was trying to keep things in her control, which sometimes meant excluding the friends and family that were trying to help guide her through this difficult time. However, they were gracious and never made me feel like I was intruding, although the situation may have seemed awkward at times. I didn't have a history with Lin, which made it easier for both of us to stay in the moment. There was no past, just the present. So, we went to her chemo treatments together, even though they weren't working any longer, and usually ordered food afterward that she did not eat. Yet she always insisted that I eat, so I did! I gained weight as fast as she was losing it! It wasn't long before she stopped chemo and entered hospice.

It was a Friday evening when I ran over to check on the caregiver who arrived at the change of shift. After I filled the caregiver in on what needed to be done through the night, Lin asked me to sit and have a glass of wine. Just like when we'd first met. This time, I sat in her red chair in my PJs next to the hospital bed, which was placed in the dining room off the foyer. (I really think she wanted the bed there to watch whoever was in her kitchen! She loved to cook and try new recipes.) Lin mentioned that she felt like she was fading. Unlike with Nan, I was able to talk to her about heaven. We laughed about how a banquet was waiting for her and how she was not picking out the menu that time! (Lin literally planned and ordered all the food for her birthday party the weekend before!) I noticed she had her nails painted red earlier that day, for Lin always liked to look nice. Since everyone turned into her friend, she managed to have the nail lady come to her house…of course!

It was raining the following Tuesday evening when I ran across the lawn for the last time. I came into her home and was greeted with the warmest hug from her family. The crackling fireplace in the den gave the foyer a radiant glow. The lights were dim and soft music was playing. Her son and daughter were by her side. I dried my tears and walked to the head of the bed, knowing our brief friendship was coming to an end. I held her face in my hands and whispered in her ear, "Good job, Lin. What a good fight! I love you, my friend." She died an hour later.

To think I almost didn't accept the first glass of wine she offered and a chance to sit a moment with a stranger. Imagine—all along I thought I was helping her, but the blessing turned out to be mine.

17

A New Generation

These days, young women and mothers have extra pressures that weren't present during my early years and certainly not during my mother-in-law's lifetime. Actually, I can't even imagine her reaction to social media. I'm certain she would not be on Facebook looking at the highlights of other people's lives. Or more disturbing, comparing herself to someone else's standards.

As for me, since I moved away from my hometown, I enjoy looking at pictures and keeping in touch this way. But I also know the importance of a phone call and time spent with a friend. After all these years, I still drive 550 miles to Great Bridge a couple of times a year to visit my girlfriends and get a hug or two. We have deep conversations, sleep overs, walks on the beach, and lunch dates. We enjoy going out in the evening and hearing local music. I consider these trips a priority in my life, and I'm already looking forward to the next one!

I watched Nan reach out to others by volunteering at her local library or bringing a warm meal to strangers through Meals on Wheels. She opened her home for anyone to stay, even stray animals. Her Schnauzers Muffin and Hoppy were two of her favorite dogs. She once had a baby pig named Arnold that stayed in the kitchen! Even though that seemed odd at the time, it makes for the best story now and an example of her caring heart.

I enjoy watching each one of my daughters-in-law show their unique ways of sharing their gifts and time with others too. It shows their caring and giving hearts. From how they decorate their homes, cook meals, visit friends, love their children, and communicate with their husbands. Each daughters-in-law's style is different from how the boys grew up, yet in the same regard, there's a lot of familiarities like love for family and friends.

In this new generation, Jeff and me finding time to spend with the kids can be a challenge since all our children live in different towns. It's not my role to dictate how they spend their time, yet I can create opportunities for everyone to gather together when possible in light of everyone's busy schedules. Is it ever perfect? No! It actually can be quite hectic at times due to all of our different opinions, likes and dislikes, personalities, school, jobs, and distance. But we are all learning as we go.

Because my oldest son, Oryan, serves in the military, his immediate family moves to a new state or country about every eighteen months. Moments with all my children together are rare, usually occurring only two times a year and lasting about three days each time. It takes the whole family, girls and guys, adjusting their schedules to make this happen. Yep, it can be chaotic to pull it together since I'm still learning that I don't have to be in charge or organize everything like when the boys were growing up. By the way, letting go, as I mentioned before, is a process, which you may have figured out in your own lives by now. I'm actually enjoying not being responsible for everything anymore. It leaves more time for other things, like traveling, playing with my grandchildren, or even, writing a book!

One of my concerns is that our family doesn't unintentionally drift apart because of distance. Our goal is to have a family getaway somewhere different every other year to reconnect. It's not possible to plan this every year right now due to Oryan and Danielle relocating so frequently. Thus, we work with the time that's available. This extra time is different than gatherings during the year at our home and is usually more costly but worth it!

One time, our getaway consisted of taking two young children and six adults on a plane to Southern California. Our getaway quickly turned into an adventure as we dragged car seats through the airport and then loaded everyone into a twelve-passenger van upon arrival in San Diego. We then drove another three hours to see our Marine and his family in the desert. Thank goodness they had done all the grocery shopping ahead of time. The guys dove into the food once we got there, which the girls are used to by now. Every man for himself!

Hopefully, these intentional efforts will provide the children and ourselves with a lot of fun memories. This new generation of women tends to be more flexible when it comes to traveling. We are definitely a family that can be spontaneous. The girls have been awesome in going with the flow. Getting a family picture is another story! You may already know how that ending goes. My input on that topic: Good luck!

No matter what size your family may be, it will always take some coordination and patience to plan a group trip. By planning menus, activities, and discussing locations the door is opened to share in something together. It's a reason for us women to text or call each other. A chance to complement ideas rather than feeling jealous. A chance to ask questions when you're unsure about something can create opportunities for honest conversations. It can prevent miscommunications or hurt feelings at times.

Along with their own parents and siblings, my daughters-in-law have created an extended family for all of us too. Sometimes there is a need to combine a family event with their sides of the family, especially the grandchildren's birthdays. To be able to gather together and enjoy each other's company is a blessing that, hopefully, you will be able to experience one day too. But an effort needs to be made by everyone to make this happen. There are usually a lot of schedules to work around. Yet, it's an effort worth making.

These days, the girls discuss questions with me and with each other in most cases. Again, investing time early on can alleviate some of the possible frustrations. It's less painful for everyone that way! I'm just giving you, the reader, a heads up.

It's definitely okay to uplift a young woman who's doing something different in this new generation instead of saying, "In my day." I have learned that if the daughters-in-law want to know how I do something or how I use to do things, they usually ask. It's something we've learned throughout the years without even realizing we do it. It's not something that happened from the beginning, yet it started occurring over time as each of us got to know one another better. I make an effort to keep in mind my earlier years when I was trying to figure things out or develop my own way of doing things. By stepping back a bit, especially as a mother-in-law, it keeps me from offering unwanted advice. My recommendations or past experiences may help or they may not. That's for her to decide.

Grace, Mercy, and Peace

As I was trying to find the words to bring this book to a close, I realized the words have already been given to me. Just as I began this story knowing who placed this topic on my heart. I understand now how God has used these years to teach me about being honest with myself. He has given me the courage to stand up for what I feel is important, even if it's only important to me. I would like to say that I knew this all along, but I didn't know.

Since Nan has been gone over these past twenty years, the memories of my time spent with her have provided me with knowledge and lessons that were designed to be shared with others. It's shedding light on the opportunities to see the women who were chosen to be in your lives differently—to hear topics and how they can possibly resonate in your situation and see each other through a new set of eyes.

Wives and mothers are usually the solid rock of the home, the heartbeat of the family. When Nan died, the heartbeat of my husband's family died too. I didn't know as a daughter-in-law that I could have helped create moments for Nan's family to continue to gather together, even if it was only a few times a year or if there was resistance and distance. It would have been a time for my children and his brothers' children to continue developing a relationship that was started by their grandmother, Nanny. She was the person to gather us all together whenever she could. These newly created moments would have been an example of bringing a family together and keeping with the simple traditions that can make a person feel like they belong to that part of the family.

My two sisters-in-law and I were all busy raising our families in different towns. They lived further out in the country, and we lived in the suburbs. I don't ever remember calling them to help Nan arrange a gathering since we didn't talk to each other outside of visiting his parents' home, although we always had a nice time together and I remember laughing a lot. Yet, the only common bond we shared was that we married brothers, and that seemed to be enough at the time. The benefit of us communicating more effectively would have later provided the family an opportunity to stay closer together after Nan passed away—a lesson well learned, for this is something I want for my family.

In the beginning, I mentioned that just seeing her boys brought her joy. As I have been writing these words over the past years and learning through my own family, I would now say, "Seeing her family together brought her joy too." I'm certain that this was also true for my own mom. But at the time, I didn't know.

My hope is that after you finish reading about my experiences, you will have a desire to invest a little time in getting to know your daughter-in-law or mother-in-law better so that early in your relationships, instead of saying, "I didn't know," you will be able to say, "Now I know." It's then that you'll find peace with each other. Like with me, time will be your teacher. Mistakes will be your lessons. What you do will speak louder than what you say. You'll be able to offer words of forgiveness much more easily. You'll be able to encourage and lift each other up, knowing that we all carry burdens. You'll be able to show or say, "I love you," to the woman God chose to put in your life. Remembering, even the little things matter and make a difference in how we respond to each other.

I looked for a photo of me and Nan to have on the last page. I searched through all the old boxes of pictures and photo albums, but there wasn't one to be found. I actually don't even remember taking one with her throughout the years. Yet in my mind and heart, I see plenty of pictures of her and I being together. There are photos of us in her kitchen, at the poolside, and bringing in clothes off the line. I see us laying across the sloshy waterbed, laughing about something from one of her romance novels. And of course, I see us enjoying a piece of dark chocolate every now and then.

Just as I remember my first glimpse of Nan when I came through the gate into her yard many years ago. I also remember the last picture of me beside her. I was on my knees, leaning my elbows on the bed, gently holding her hand as she slipped away. In a photograph, there are no words, yet this particular picture in my mind and heart speaks to me often.

I tried to recall if she ever said, "I love you," to me, but I cannot think of a time I heard those words from her. But I can recall the grace she gave me when I didn't know. I can recall the mercy she gave me when needed if I said or did something careless. Most importantly, I can recall the peace she gave me as a young woman and mother. Now I know that these are all the ways love can be extended to others without saying a word.

While reading this book back to myself, I understand why I didn't need to hear I love you from her at the time. Because I felt her love for me all along through the way she treated me with respect and kindness. I can only hope that she felt the same from me.

Without knowing it, this imperfect lady whom I called Nan left a legacy. She and I were drawn together only by her son, and that's okay. Through her example and over time, I've learned the importance of communicating more effectively with my daughters-in-law, and I'm sharing that information with you. It's not a competition for our sons' hearts because as their mothers, we are still loved by them in a special way and always will be. Your son may even develop a new sense of admiration towards you as he sees the care and patience you extend to his wife.

The challenge comes from within us to choose to get along and consider each other's feelings as women, with the common goal of becoming the daughters-in-law and mothers-in-law you would want to have one day. It will come full circle. It has for me. My hope is that your lives, your family's lives, and the next generation of mother- in-law and daughter-in-law relationships may continue to grow, or at least get a little better.

I recently visited the white concrete house in the country and stood out back on the red porch. The paint is now cracked. The wood is splintered, and the side railings have been taken down. As I stood and looked at the yard, I closed my eyes so I could hear the splashing of the pool and see the hammock swinging under the big shade tree. I could smell the smoke coming from the rusty burn barrel. In the pasture, the horses were eating grass, and out at the barn, the guys were standing around having a beer together "talking trash." Meanwhile, on the side of the yard, the swing set was creaking as Nanny's grandchildren played care freely and Sweet Pea the goat was chopping on the scraps from our lunch that were thrown over the fence. In the same area, the chickens were running around clucking as if something was chasing them. The feel of the sun on my face felt so warm and familiar as I stood on the old back porch.

Finally, I opened my eyes, to see an empty yard. The pool was gone and the old shade tree that had fallen years before and had been replaced by green grass. The barn was weathered and in need of repair. All the horses had been buried in the pasture and the burn barrel sat alone in the yard, empty.

I stepped off the porch to leave, slowly walking to the metal fence on the side of the house where I entered into the yard many years before. As I turned to look back, I noticed the clothesline was still standing. This time, I didn't need to close my eyes to see the image of Nan standing in her shorts, white tank top, and boots up to her calf. The smile on her face will always be my first impression of the woman I called Nan. I smiled back at the memory as I let myself out of the fenced yard. While walking away, I heard the metal gate clink shut once more. Softly I whispered to myself, "Until we meet again Nan, on the other side."

Epilogue

To write this epilogue, I literally had to look up the meaning of this word. As I mentioned, I'm not a writer. What started off twenty years ago with a poem and journaling evolved into a story inspired by a woman I called Nan.

One definition of an epilogue is that it can be used to allow the main character to speak freely. In this case, the main character, Nan is not here to describe her experience of being a mother-in-law.

So, I went to another definition of an epilogue where the meaning of the book's title is revealed. *I Called Her Nan* is about a woman who was both my mother-in-law and friend, who over-time made an impact on my life. Yet the impact wasn't felt until I started walking in her shoes, shoes that have since taken me through the mud of disappointments and tears of many kinds. Shoes that have allowed me to appreciate the joys in my life and to understand how she must have enjoyed those moments too. Shoes that became worn by working and serving others. Most importantly, her shoes weren't perfectly made, yet they had strong soles that allowed her to walk with her family through all the seasons of their lives and her own. I'm proud to wear the shoes Nan left behind. My desire is to remove the dirt that I keep stepping in at times as I navigate my way through the relationships with my daughters-in-law, ultimately polishing them up through words of encouragement, patience, and wisdom. I want the shoes that are handed down to look new and feel fresh for Danielle, Megan, and Nicki as they slip them on to start their own journeys one day.

The last definition for an epilogue is that it can be the final chapter at the end of a story that often serves to reveal the fates of the characters. My hope is that you as the reader find yourself as one of the characters in the center of this book. That your ears heard and your eyes saw new ways to communicate more effectively as a daughter-in- law and as a mother-in-law. Our fate and relationships depend on that communication and acceptance of the differences in each other.

The end of this story belongs to all of you who have taken the time to read this book. However, don't be surprised if it takes the next twenty years to figure out the ending. You are the writer of your own story. Make it worth sharing!

I'll help you get started.

A Simple Exercise

My name is _____

I am the daughter-in-law/mother-in-law to:

_____

The first time I met her, I thought:

_____

_____

Our common bond is:

_____

_____

So far, our relationship is:

_____

_____

The name I plan on calling my mother-in-law is

_____

Learning About Each Other

Before you begin this section, I suggest you take the time to grab lunch/coffee together and find out these things about each other.

Daughters-in law (to be), ask your husband/fiance questions about his mom ahead of time. This way you can hear his impression of the woman who raised him.

_____

_____

Mothers, ask your son questions about his (future) wife.

_____

_____

Some of her interest and hobbies:

_____

_____

Some of the things we have in common:

_____

_____

Things I admire about her:

_____

_____

Some frustrations I have experienced:

_____

_____

Differences I have noticed:

_____

_____

I realize that I need to work on:

_____

_____

My relationship goal to have with my mother-in-law/ daughter-in-law:

_____

_____

I think my son/husband seeing both of us women communicating better will make him feel:

_____

_____

Blessings from a Mother's heart, Cathy

Acknowledgements

To my daughters-in-law, Danielle, Megan, and Nicki:

As women, we all have many roles in life with people who depend on us to be a wives, daughters, mothers, and friends. I want to thank each of you for being a daughter and friend to me.

I wish I could say that I picked you, but I now see that God picked each of you specifically to be mine for this added role in my life as daughters-in-law.

The general image and anticipation of mothers-in-law and daughters-in-law were created by women from past generations, which can make these future relationships potentially uncertain from the start. Of course, it depends on who's story you hear. I came into my own role as a mother-in-law excited about the promise of a new relationship, which I now see created expectations on my end. Somehow, I forgot that just because you were marrying my sons didn't mean that we would agree about everything or that you would have picked me if given the choice.

Initially, although we were hopeful when we met and our first impressions went well, we found out before long that it takes time to actually learn about each other, especially when starting from scratch. Just like anything in life that has true value, it takes patience, sacrifice, and work. Through perseverance, the reward of choosing to work towards having a healthy relationship will resonate within our families and possibly be an example to those around us.

I could not have written this book without your input and support, even if you were just going along with it sometimes. I believe this book will provide an opportunity to create a new generation of mothers-in-law and daughters-in-law stories. My hope is that it will benefit those starting their married life or provide encouragement to those in need of a new perspective.

Over time, I have genuinely grown to love each one of you girls for the women you are and not just because you married into this family. Thank you for loving my boys so well, creating a home for them, and providing Jeff and me with beautiful grandchildren! Thank you for choosing to not just tolerate me but to care for my feelings, which makes me feel loved.

To Kristen, Brittany, Nikki, Kirsten, Lynn, and Heidi:

Thank you for investing your time listening to me over the months I worked to pull this together. Your encouragement resonates throughout the book. Your suggestions lead me to elaborate into areas that were pertinent to the stories. Your viewpoints gave me insight where I could not see.

Kristen, your friendship allowed me to pour out my heart. I'll be forever grateful.

To my family and friends:

Hopefully each of you can see between the lines and pages of this book. I'm certain that you will see yourselves in one of the many memories that have been told. You may remember a location that was mentioned or moments that we shared together. At times, you may find yourselves reminiscing on your personal journey through some of the stories mentioned. Hopefully, they will make you laugh or at least smile. Know that I value and love each of you for the unique role you have in my life.

To my mother, Eleanor, and sister Cindy:

I love you both.

To Jeff, Oryan, Morgan, and Jordan:

My husband, Jeff, and my three sons, a special thank you for putting up with my silliness throughout the years and for loving me regardless. You guys have always encouraged me whenever I tried something new, and your support has been priceless!

I could write stories that would go on and on about the years we had together as a family of five. But I'll spare the tarradiddles and details in order to maintain my image of being somewhat put together. Shhh.

I'm grateful for our family, and I feel blessed with so much more than I deserve. I'll love each of you forever!

To Jim, Morgan, Makenzie and Hannah:

From the website, editing, cover design, and lay out, each of your unique gifts brings my vision to life! Thank you for making the publication of this book possible!